The Sayings of Samuel Pepys

Henry —

with love from

Richard and Julian

Christmas Eve 2005

The Sayings Series

Jane Austen
Lord Byron
Winston Churchill
Charles Dickens
Benjamin Disraeli
F. Scott Fitzgerald
Benjamin Franklin
Thomas Hardy
Henrik Ibsen
Dr Johnson
James Joyce
John Keats
Rudyard Kipling
D.H. Lawrence
Somerset Maugham
Friedrich Nietzsche
George Orwell
Dorothy Parker
Samuel Pepys
Ezra Pound
Sir Walter Scott
William Shakespeare
George Bernard Shaw
Sydney Smith
R.L. Stevenson
Jonathan Swift
Leo Tolstoy
Anthony Trollope
Mark Twain
Oscar Wilde
Virginia Woolf
W.B. Yeats
The Bible
The Buddha
Jesus
Moses
Muhammad

The Sayings of

SAMUEL
PEPYS

edited by
Richard Ollard

DUCKWORTH

First published in 1996 by
Gerald Duckworth & Co. Ltd.
The Old Piano Factory
48 Hoxton Square, London N1 6PB
Tel: 0171 729 5986
Fax: 0171 729 0015

Introduction and editorial arrangement
© 1996 by Richard Ollard

A catalogue record for this book is available
from the British Library

ISBN 0 7156 2667 1

Typeset by Ray Davies
Printed in Great Britain by
Redwood Books Ltd., Trowbridge

Contents

7 Introduction

13 Personal Philosophy

15 Enjoyment & Pleasures

19 Music & Painting

22 Religion & Conscience

24 Scepticism & Credulity

28 The Sea & Seamen

34 Trade & Navigation

36 The Navy

42 Politics & Public Affairs

46 Marriage & Family Life

49 Money

52 Writing Letters

55 Descriptive Reporting

59 History

61 Patriotism & National Character

62 Illness & Old Age

Sources and abbreviations

D = *The Diary of Samuel Pepys* ed. R.C. Latham and W. Matthews, 11 vols. (1970-83).

FC = *Further Correspondence of Samuel Pepys* ed. J.R. Tanner (1929).

FL = *The Letters of Samuel Pepys and his Family Circle* ed. H.T. Heath (1955).

Howarth = *Letters and the Second Diary of Samuel Pepys* ed. R.G. Howarth (1932).

LBK = National Maritime Museum: Pepys Letterbook.

NM = *Samuel Pepys Naval Minutes* ed. J.R. Tanner (1926).

PC = *Private Correspondence and Miscellaneous Papers of Samuel Pepys* ed. J.R. Tanner, 2 vols. (1926).

Rawl = Bodleian Library Rawlinson MSS.

T = *Tangier Papers of Samuel Pepys* ed. E. Chappell (1935).

Note: Square brackets – [   ] – indicate an editorial insertion

Introduction

Pepys is by general consent the greatest
diarist in our literature. But, prominent
though he was in the life of England in the
second half of the seventeenth century, no
one suspected that this was to be his title to
immortality. No one, in fact, knew that he
was keeping a diary at all. He took good
care that they should not since its contents,
in hostile hands, would have been highly
dangerous.

But the diary, which from start to finish
covers only eight and a half years of his
young manhood, is by no means the sole,
or even the main, record of his thoughts
and opinions. For nearly twenty-five years,
first as Clerk of the Acts to the Navy Board
and then as Secretary to the Board of
Admiralty, he was at the centre of affairs.
The Navy was by far the largest spending
department. The Second and Third Dutch
Wars, during both of which Pepys was in
office, were perhaps the hardest-fought in
our history. A stream of letters, of
instructions, of reports, of enquiry, of
reproof poured from his pen. A pioneer of
administrative efficiency, he kept file
copies of everything he wrote. Besides this
vast business correspondence – none of it
faceless, indeed most of it strongly marked
by the impress of his personality – Pepys

was assiduous in keeping in touch with his family and with the circle of learned men whom he met both as a Fellow of the Royal Society and as an active patron of the arts and of scholarship.

There is thus a wealth of material from which to extract his sayings. Since the Diary is far and away the best known source I have drawn on it sparingly. There is already an admirable selection from it *A Pepys Anthology*, compiled by its editor, Robert Latham and his wife Linnet, which confines itself strictly to this source. Clearly to neglect it altogether would be perverse. It would largely exclude important aspects of Pepys's mentality, notably his unrivalled gift for descriptive reporting and his intimate reflections on marriage and domestic life.

Since his chief concern for the greater part of his active life was the management of naval affairs and the development of what might be called a naval philosophy, that is the consideration of maritime affairs in relation to the history of this country and to its current and probable interests, I have given that the lion's share. But I have tried also to indicate the extraordinary multiplicity of his intellectual and artistic interests. These were all very much part of the man, as he himself emphasised in his choice of motto, *Mens cujusque is est quisque*, Man's essential self is his mind.

Pepys's characteristic expression is not epigrammatic. Capable as he was of pithy, witty, searching remarks, his preference was for the orotund, the long, unhurried sentence, branching off into parentheses and even parentheses within parentheses, but always rejoining a main clause that is often coterminous with a paragraph. I have sometimes butchered these into more easily assimilated form, making it plain where this has been done. But it would be to falsify the cast of his mind, his love of decorum and proper formality, not to include some passages in which the measured, careful tones of a man who could not abide sluttishness or disorder can be heard without interruption.

When quoting from unprinted manuscript sources I have modernised spelling and punctuation but not always capitalisation. Where passages quoted are in print I have followed the usage there employed. A slight inconsistency seems to me a small price to pay for the avoidance of pedantry and for the highest degree of fidelity to the original that can be achieved without making unnecessary difficulties for a modern reader.

The extracts from the Diary are dated because that provides the easiest form of reference. Otherwise I have not supplied dates though the entries are in general in chronological sequence in so far as this can be established.

What sort of man emerges from this gathering of his observations? The breadth of his personality enables every reader to perceive an outline for himself. Pepys's response to life, especially to its beauties, is immediate and strong. It is this that has made him a favourite with posterity. At the same time he is far removed from Dr Pangloss, believing that all is for the best in the best of all possible worlds. Squalor, poverty, distress touch him but he accepts them, as he accepted ill-health and acute pain in his own life, as evils beyond his power to remove but not, for that reason, to be allowed to dominate the sovereign independence of his own mind. Pepys is always and everywhere his own man. He cannot be taken over by a party or by any prescriptive philosophy or creed. He belongs, no one more profoundly, to the English tradition of empiricism, of seeing whether something works in practice rather than whether it fits into some general theory offering an intellectually satisfactory explanation of phenomena.

It is this combination of down-to-earth matter-of-factness with the instincts of a hedonist and the perceptions of an aesthete that makes the range of his sympathies both so extraordinary and so communicable. Pepys is at one and the same time both Everyman and a quite outstandingly observant and acute critic of Everyman's experiences. It is the same with his politics and with his religion. Charles II and his brother who succeeded him as James II in 1685 had no more

devoted and no more effective servant
than Pepys, but, as readers of the Diary
know, he was their most devastating critic.
In religion he was a lifelong member of the
Church of England and a lifelong
anti-clerical, hardly finding a good word to
say of the bishops or of the many
clergymen whose ministrations he so
sedulously attended, often by his own
account in a worldly not to say carnal state
of mind.

The same comprehensiveness can be
found in his professional life. In his early
years as a public servant he took bribes on
a substantial scale, though always
justifying himself by the alleged happy
coincidence of these offerings with the best
bargain available in whatever commodity
market the deal was done. Later he took a
high moral tone in these matters,
reproving people who approached him
with such incentives and firmly denying
professional advancement to friends and
relations who made their personal
connexion the grounds of their application.
The same is true again in his sexual morals
and in his attitude to the class structure.
The sincerity of his belief that husband and
wife should be faithful to each other
co-exists with the candour that reveals his
enjoyment of his own infidelities. The
society of his day was clearly stratified by
birth. Pepys recognises this as a fact to be
taken into account in the ordinary
transactions of life, not least in raising the

status of the sea-officers and allowing the maritime interests of the country their proper weight in the conduct of national affairs. But unlike many of his contemporaries he never thought the worse of a man because his father was a drayman or the better because he was cousin to an Earl.

There is only one note that never sounds in his life and in his thoughts and that is boredom. The world, its inhabitants, its beauties, its arts, its business, never ceased to engage his interest and to elicit a reaction.

As his friend John Evelyn remarked in a letter written when they were both old men, '*O Fortunate Mr Pepys*! who knows, possesses and injoyes all that's worth the seeking after. Let me live among your inclinations and I shall be happy.'

Personal Philosophy

… a strange slavery that I stand in to beauty, that I value nothing near it.

D, 6 September 1664

Lay very long in bed, discoursing with Mr Hill of most things of a man's life, and how little merit doth prevail in the world, but only favour – and that for myself, chance without merit brought me in, and that diligence only keeps me so, and will, living as I do among so many lazy people, that the diligent man becomes necessary, that they cannot do anything without him.

D, 1 November 1665

… as I was at leisure, I … did try to make a Song in the prayse of a Liberall genius (as I take my own to be) to all studies and pleasures; but it not proving to my mind, I did reject it and so proceed not in it.

D, 3 November 1661

… Nothing which has yet or may further happen towards the rendering me more conspicuous in the world, has led or can ever lead to the admitting any alteration in the little methods of my private way of living, as having not in my nature any more aversion to sordidness than I have to pomp, and in particular that sort of it which consists in the length and trouble of such a train (I mean of servants for state only) ....

Howarth, pp. 48-9

My aim is for the good of futurity, though little deserving it of me.

NM, 215

The truth is, I do indulge myself a little the more pleasure, knowing that this is the proper age of my life to do it, and out of my observation that most men that do thrive in the world do forget to take pleasure during the time that they are getting their estate but reserve that till they have got one, and then it is too late for them to enjoy it with any pleasure.

D, 10 March 1666

For against a Lyar the best defence in the world is to obtaine the most you can of his Discourse; because let his memory be never so good, if he gives himselfe the Liberty of talking much he cannot avoid discovering himself.

FL, 86

For (I thank God) I have alwaies carried about me Such a watchfulness and Integrity as will Support me, (with God's assistance), against any thing that the Malice of Mankind can offer to my prejudice.

FL, 91

Enjoyments & Pleasures

Up by 4 a-clock in the morning and read
Cicero's *Second Oracion against Cataline*,
which pleased me exceedingly; and more I
discern therein than ever I thought was to
be found in him. But I perceive it was my
ignorance, and that he is as good a writer
as ever I read in my life.

D, 13 June 1662

To St Paul's Churchyard to my booksellers;
and having gained this day in the office, by
my stationer's bill to the King, about 40s.
or £3, I did sit here two or three hours,
calling for twenty books to lay this money
out upon; and found myself at a great loss
where to choose, and do see how my
nature would gladly returne to the laying
out of money in this trade. I could not tell
whether to lay out my money for books of
pleasure, as plays, which my nature was
most earnest in; but at last, after seeing
Chaucer, Dugdales *History of Pauls*, Stow's
London, Gesner, *History of Trent*, besides
Shakespeare, Johnson and Beaumonts
plays, I at last chose Dr Fuller's *Worthy's*,
The Cabbala or Collections of Letters of State –
and a little book, *Delices de Hollande*, with
another little book or two, all of good use
or serious pleasure; and *Hudibras*, both
parts, the book now in the greatest Fashion

for drollery, though I cannot, I confess, see
enough where the wit lies.

D, 10 December 1663

All day at the office but a little at dinner;
and there till past 12. So home to bed,
pleased as I always am after I have rid a
great deal of work, it being very
satisfactory to me.   D, 6 May 1665

We spent most of the morning talking and
reading of *The Seige of Rhodes* [an opera by
Davenant], which is certainly (the more I
read it the more I think so) the best poem
that ever was wrote ... But Lord, the mirth
it caused to me to be waked in the night by
their Snoaring round about me – I did
laugh till I was ready to burst.

D, 1 October 1665

Thence to the Change, and to the Sun
behind it to dinner with the Lieutenant of
the Tower and Collonell Norwood and
others – where strange pleasure they seem
to take in their wine and meat, and
discourse of it with the curiosity and joy
that methinks was below men of worth.

D, 9 February 1666

Here stayed till 9 a-clock almost, and then
took coach, with so much love and
kindness from my Lady Carteret, Lady
Jemimah, and Lady Slaning, that it joys my
heart (and when I consider the manner of
my going hither, with a coach and four
horses, and servants and a woman with us,

and coming hither, being so much made of, and used with that state, and then going to Windsor and being shown all that we were there, and had wherewith to give everybody something for their pains, and then going home, and all in fine weather, and no fears nor cares upon me, I do think myself obliged to think myself happy, and do look upon myself at this time in the happiest occasion a man can be; and whereas we take pains in expectation of future comfort and ease, I have taught myself to reflect upon myself at present as happy and enjoy myself in that consideration, and not only please myself with thoughts of future wealth, and forget the pleasures we at present enjoy).

D, 28 February 1666

God forgive me, I do still see that my nature is not to be quite conquered, but will esteem pleasure above all things; though, yet in the middle of it, it hath reluctancy after my business, which is neglected by my following my pleasure. However, music and women I cannot but give way to, whatever my business is.

D, 9 March 1666

Up, and at my chamber all the morning and the office, doing business and also reading a little of *L'Escolle des Filles*, which is a mighty lewd book, but yet not amiss for a sober man once to read over to inform himself in the villainy of the world.

D, 9 February 1668

On the conditions of a private library

... Wherein what I propose principally to
be attended to is,
1. As to the General Scope and Purpose of
it:
    The comprehending in fewest Books
    and least Room the greatest diversity of
    SUBJECTS, STILES and LANGUAGES its
    Owner's Reading will bear; with
    Reguard had to theyr AUTHORS,
    EDITIONS, and PROPORTIONS on each
    subject, answerable to theyr Weight, and
    the particular Genius of their said owner.
2. In the Book-binder's Worke
    Decency and Uniformity: with some
    Marke of theyr Propriety [i.e. ownership]
3. In theyr Registry
    Clearness, Comprehensiveness and
    Order ....

PC, ii.247-8

Music & Painting

I played also, which I have not done this long time before on any instrument; and at last broke up and I to my office a little while, being fearful of being too much taken with musique, for fear of returning to my old dotage thereon and so neglect my business as I used to do.

D, 17 February 1663

Here the best company for Musique I ever was in in my life, and wish I could live and die in it, both for music and the face of Mrs Pierce and my wife and Knipp, who is pretty enough, but the most excellent mad-humoured thing; and sings the noblest that ever I heard in my life, and Rolt with her, some things together most excellently – I spent the night in an ecstasy almost.

D, 6 December 1665

To the King's House to see Virgin Martyr ... not that the play is worth much, but it is finely acted by Becke Marshall; but that which did please me beyond anything in the whole world was the wind-musique when the Angell comes down, which is so sweet that it ravished me; and endeed, in a word, did wrap up my soul so that it made me really sick, just as I have formerly been when in love with my wife; that neither then nor all the evening going home and at home, I was able to think of anything, but remained all night transported, so that I could not believe that ever any music hath that real command over the soul of a man as this did upon me, and makes me resolve to practise wind-music and to make my wife do the like.

D, 27 February 1668

Musick, a science peculiarly productive of a pleasure that no state of life, publick or private, secular or sacred; no difference of age or season; no temper of mind or condition of health exempt from present anguish; nor, lastly, distinction of quality, renders either improper, untimely or unentertaining.

PC, ii.109.

To Hales's to see my wife's picture, which I like mighty well; and there had the pleasure to see how suddenly he draws the Heavens, laying a dark ground and then lightening it when and where he will.

D, 19 March 1666

Thence to Hales's to see how my father's picture goes on, which pleases me mighty well, though I find again … that a picture may have more of likeness in the first or second working than it shall have when finished; though this is very well and to my full content; but so it is. And contrarily, mine was not so like at the first, second or third sitting as it was afterward.

D, 18 June 1666

To Mr Cooper's house [Samuel Cooper,
the miniaturist] to see some of his work;
which is all in little, but so excellent, as
though I must confess I do think the
colouring of the flesh to be a little forced,
yet the painting is so extraordinary, as I do
never expect to see the like again.

D, 30 March 1668

To Mr Streeter's the famous history painter
... and there I found him and Dr Wren and
several virtuosos looking upon the
paintings which he is making for the new
theatre at Oxford [the Sheldonian]; and
endeed they look as if they would be very
fine, and the rest thinks better than those
of Rubens in the Banqueting-house at
Whitehall, but I do not so fully think so –
but they will certainly be very noble.

D, 1 February 1669

What sea-scape of our own nation have we
ever had like Vanderveld or others?

NM, 407

Never any pictures to be met with among
us, either ancient or modern, of persons of
any quality drawn in the habit of seamen,
but all as soldiers or in some other dress.

NM, 196

Religion & Conscience

He that makes Reason his guide goes by a law of God's making, subject to no falsifications and misconstructions which all other guides whether written or others, are and must necessarily be.

Rawl A 171, f. 217

Whence it is that Mrs Hayward appears so little satisfied with what has been done for her I know not, nor am very solicitous to know, as having all the satisfaction I wish for in my consciousness of having done all I could for her service, and my readiness to do more as I have opportunity, whether she knows or thinks so or no; there being no less due from me to the memory and merit of her husband.

LBK, f. 708

Then to my mother again; and after supper she and I talked very high about religion, I in defence of the religion I was born in.

D, 4 March 60

[On board the *Naseby*] I and Will Howe, the surgeon, parson, and Balty supped in the Lieutenant's cabin and afterwards sat disputing, the parson and I against extempory prayer very hot.

D, 8 April 60

[On giving up the keeping of his Diary]
And so I betake myself to that course
which is almost as much as to see myself
go into my grave – for which, and all the
discomforts that will accompany my being
blind, the good God prepare me.

D, 31 May 1669

Walked into [St James's] Park to the
Queen's chapel and there heard a good
deal of their mass and some of their
musique, which is not so contemptible, I
think, as our people would make it, it
pleasing me very well – and indeed, better
than the anthemne I heard afterward at
Whitehall at my coming back. I stayed till
the King went down to receive the
Sacrament, and stood in his closett with a
great many others and there saw him
receive it – which I did never see the
manner of before. But do see very little
difference between the degree of the
ceremonies used by our people in the
administration thereof and that in the
Roman church, saving that methought our
chapel was not so fine, nor the manner of
doing it so glorious, as it was in the
Queenes chapel.

D, 15 April 1666

Scepticism & Credulity

Noah's Ark must needs be made of some extraordinary timber and plank that could remain good after having been an hundred years in building, whereas our thirty new ships [a building programme of which Pepys was very proud] are some of them rotten within less than five. Moreover Mr Shere computes from its dimensions that six months would have sufficed to have built what Moses assigns an hundred years for. And enquire also how carpenters and caulkers came to be found, if she was the first ship; what account could be given of all that ado for the preserving of one little family ... and lastly how they all agreed (contrary to all humane practice in like cases of distress ...) to see this means of safety enjoyed by so few persons, and oxen and asses, suffering the universality of mankind to perish without contention for a share in it.

NM, 206

This only I shall not now spare to say; That as to the business of the second sight, I little expected to have been ever brought so near to a conviction of the reality of it as by your Lordship's and the Lord Tarbutt's authoritys I must already own myself to be.

Not that I yet know how to subscribe to my Lord Tarbutt's charging it upon some singularity of quality in the air or eye of the persons affected therewith. Forasmuch as I have never heard of other consequences of any indisposure in the medium or organs of sight than what related to the miscolouring, misfiguring, diminishing, or undue magnifying of an object truly existing and exposed thereto. Whereas in this case we are entertained with daggers, shrouds, arrows, gibbets, and God knows what, that indeed are not; and consequently must be the creatures of the mind only (however directed to them) and not of the eye.

Nor yet, as to the reality of this effect, would I be thought, my Lord, to derive this propension of mine to the belief of it, to the credit only which I find it to have obtained among your neighbours the Highlanders; for that it has been my particular fortune to have outlived the belief of another point of faith relating to the eyes, no less extraordinary, nor of less universal reception elsewhere, than this can be in Scotland. I mean, the *mal de ojo* [the evil eye] in Spain; with a third touching the sanative and prophetick faculty of the *Saludadores* [self-proclaimed miracle workers: in modern Spanish the word means quack doctors] there. As having heretofore pursued my enquirys thereinto so far upon the place, as to have fully convinced myself of the vanity thereof, especially of the latter, from the very confessions of its professors.

At the office in the morning and did business. By and By we are called to Sir W. Batten to see the strange creature that Capt. Holmes hath brought with him from Guiny; it is a great baboone, but so much like a man in most things, that (though they say there is a species of them) yet I cannot believe but that it is a monster got of a man and a she-baboone. I do believe it already understands much English; and I am of the mind it might be taught to speak or make signs.

D, 24 August 1661

At noon to my Lord Crewes – where one Mr Templer (an ingenious [man] and a person of honour he seems to be) dined; and discoursing of the nature of serpents, he told us of some that in the waste places of Lancashire do grow to a great bigness, and that do feed upon larkes, which they take thus – they observe when the lark is soared to the highest, and do crawle till they come to be just underneath them; and there they place themselfs with their mouths uppermost, and there (as is conceived) they do eject poyson up to the bird; for the bird doth suddenly come down again in its course of a circle, and falls directly into the mouth of the serpent – which is very strange.

D, 4 February 1662

… That mighty mystery the world does so
grope after in open day, that shews
nothing to me more obvious than (not only
the certainty) but inevitableness of a war.
But if faith be only the evidence of things
not seen, infidelity must be a
non-discerning of things visible.

FC, 318

And therefore by the way pray learne of
mee this one Lesson, which on this
Occasion I have Observed not onely you
but others of Our Friends, not to have yet
met with, vizt. To bee most Slow to believe
what we most wish should bee true.

FL, 115

The Sea & Seamen

England has taken a knight-errant, St George, for its guardian saint, and not any of the Apostles and other fishermen that would have had more relation to the sea.

NM, 167

Observe the maliciousness of our English proverb towards the service of the sea, viz – That the sea and the gallows refused nobody. Which is verified too much in our practice of sending none thither but the vicious or poor.

NM, 62

The ignorant censures of men at land have made many of our bravest men desperate, to their destruction at sea.

NM, 23

Observable that the smallest wages given by the Crown in the time of King Edward the 3rd to any sort of people borne upon the King's books was to the seamen, his very fiddlers having 4 times as much, and that the seaman's wages remains the same upon the King's books from that to King Edward the 6th, though others (I believe) would be found to have been advanced.

NM, 65

But when it comes to require real drudgery
and constant toil, as the seaman's trade
now does, we could not endure it so well
as other nations and particularly the Dutch
do.

NM, 83

Observe also that in '88, there was a
nobleman Admiral, they were fain to make
two plain tarpaulins, Drake and Hawkyns,
their Vice- and Rear-Admirals,
notwithstanding there were a great many
men of quality in the fleet, and more
followed them in ships hired by
themselves. But of what service their
inexperience could be (more than to show
their prowess) is easy to be judged.

NM, 119

The seamen are the most adventurous
creatures in the world, and the most free of
their money after all their dangers when
they come to receive it.

NM, 148

I know nothing taken from the sea into
common use among people of quality but
the word *Huzzah*, and whence comes that,
and how laudably applied?

NM, 166

Thom Killegrew's [playwright and theatre
manager] father used to cry to his wife
'Lord, sweetheart, here's Thom come home
again!' *viz.* after several times sending him
to sea for his viciousness, to be rid of him.

NM, 166

The less wonder that our admirals and
great seamen have rarely, if ever, raised
estates by it; for that their employment
generally keeps them at distance out of
sight, and out of the way of soliciting their
private profit, while others at home have
therein all the advantage of them. The
seaman's services also are by this means
not seen.

NM, 191

Seamen are used to danger, and so not
confounded upon any surprises of danger,
by which 20 of them are in such case of
more use than 100 not so accustomed.

NM, 250

Englishmen, and more especially seamen,
love their bellies above anything else, and
therefore it must always be remembered in
the management of the victualling of the
Navy that to make any abatement from
them in the quantity or agreeableness of
the victuals is to discourage and provoke
them in the tenderest point, and will
sooner render them disgusted with the
King's service than any other hardship that
can be put upon them.

NM, 250

Will not the constant and evident hazards
of a seaman's life, and the odds therefore
of their dying untimely deaths, go a long
way towards atoning for the general
libertinism and unthriftiness of their lives,
at least towards the shewing the

unlikelihood of that trade's raising many families to wealth (as others do) were the profits to be made thereby greater than they at the best are now known to be?

NM, 255

Were it not to be wished that the seamen's trade might be made so honourable and profitable, as that not only the younger brothers of England might be encouraged to seek their fortunes that way, as they hitherto have generally done (at home and abroad) by trailing of a pike, etc., in landservice, for the sake of the latter; but that even the elder might esteem it, for the dignity of it, no diminution to their qualities or estates (whatever they may be) to do the same for a voyage or two, but on the contrary have it solemnly made a principal (if not a necessary) step towards their advancement to the greatest offices of State and Court, and to carry with it the public credit of being one of the first qualifications in a nobleman or gentleman for public trust, in Parliament or elsewhere, to have taken this degree in that great article of our English government (hitherto so little understood and so dearly paid for) which relates to the sea, and the truth as well as importance of its interest therein.

NM, 405-6

Take notice that in the framing of our prayers for the sea, our bishops being land men have made no provision for praying for a fair wind, or any wind at all upon a calm, or any other of the many evils incident to the sea, but only against storms and enemies, and thanks only for deliverance from those two.

T, 109-10

It is remarkable that Colonel Wyndham is the only gentleman of estate that ever was known to addict himself to the sea only for his pleasure in any age, having never been in any service at sea either merchant or the King's, but only do what he has done for pleasure and from his own natural addiction.

T, 110

What can show more the difficulty of the seaman's life than that no man will stay in it longer than he has got an estate that is competent like our ordinary masters of ships, and that no man that has so much learning of any kind as he thinks he can get a living with, will stay there or go thither, but keep on shore. So that the whole generality of those that go and stay there are either poor or illiterate or desperate people, or at least such as being by force or chance brought thither by times are by custom hardened in it, and knowing no better way, continue it.

T, 220

I know nothing that can give a better notion of infinity and eternity than being upon the sea in a little vessel without anything in sight but yourself within the whole hemisphere.

T, 224

Trade & Navigation

First and remote discoveries may be kept
secret, especially where it is worth the
charge of providing against the approach
of strangers, as it is to the Spaniards in
America. But where nations do traffic one
with another, as they do here, it is
impossible.

NM, 4

London has always been a great
emporium, and therefore the road to it
must have always been publicly known.

NM, 31

That other nations came very anciently
hither to trade with us does not at all prove
us but them to be navigators; no more than
our going now to the East and West Indies
proves the Indians to be so; and that was
our case, I doubt.

NM, 70

Is not our prohibiting of old the
exportation of horses one full instance of
the long ignorance of this nation in the
good of its own trade?

NM, 192

Of the four great discoverers, we the last
and least.

NM, 223

Enquire and consider what we have of any art or trade either of English invention or growth that deserves to be, or either is, forbidden to be published to strangers.

NM, 227

Art [Pepys is speaking here of the art of navigation] is not an advantage particular to us, it being common to all other nations equal to us, but labour and experience; this making men diligent and painful, whilst art makes them rather idle, proud, and opiniate; and experience it is we must boast of at sea or nothing. More artists miscarry at sea (through their idleness and presumption) than men of experience less knowing.

NM, 228

The Navy

The life of a virtuous officer in the Navy
[i.e. an administrator, such as Pepys
himself, as distinct from what he would
have called a sea-officer] is a continual war
defensive, viz. against the Ministers of
State, and in particular the Lord
Treasurers, in time of peace, and all
prejudiced inquisitors and malcontents
with the Navy management in time of war;
the former grudging every penny of
money almost that is spent, and so keeping
it short and postponing it to all other
occasions in all the means either of
repairing the ships, building of new, laying
up of stores, or executing any of its good
laws for preserving of discipline by the
protection which the breakers of them find
from some or other friends of potency at
Court. While on the other hand, during
war its Officers are not only left to shift for
themselves but have it expected from them
by the Court to find ways of imposing
upon the world the belief of all things
being well in the Navy, the supplies of
money plentiful, and the work done. And
if they cannot succeed in it, but by the
plainness of their misconduct are rendered
unjustifiable, are delivered over to the
inquisitors, and those only of them left to
bear the burthen of all, that in their
particular places best deserved of the

Commonwealth, by having both done and suffered most towards the reproving and remedying what was indeed amiss, and in the contending for and doing the little that was otherwise.

NM, 264-5

The word 'Navy' should be the Englishman's Tetragrammaton and be held no less sacred with him than the other known one among the Jews.

NM, 322

Is there any one good rule in our Navy that has not been long established in France? And are there not many in theirs which we have not?

NM, 356

Among other things, it pleased me to have it demonstrated that a purser without professed cheating is a professed loser, twice as much as he gets.

D, 22 November 1665

It is high time for us to assert frugality to the highest officers if we ever would expect to have it practised among the meanest.

LBK, 536

[To his cousin Charles Pepys, a dockyard officer]
But above all let me recommend it to you to avoid the thinking that whatever it is you owe either to him [Commissioner Gregory] or me on this occasion, either he or I would have stirred one step for you upon the single score of your Relation to me had it not been seconded with the opinion we both have of your Desire as well as Ability to perform the work of your Place, and that you will not only continue to express the same by all ways of Diligence, Sobriety and Faithfulness, but that you will rectify that Lowness of Spirit and Backwardness in appearing in the execution of your Duty, as a Warrant Officer, which (without any other Crime) had, but for the seasonable kindness of Commissioner Gregory certainly undone you: your submitting yourself to be imposed upon in your Office by your Inferior having given him an opportunity of carrying away the credit of all that was done, and you to be looked upon as a Cypher. ...

Rawl A 170, f. 26

[Notes in Pepys's hand of a conference with James II and Godolphin at which the re-modelling of naval administration was discussed.]
Navy General Considerations
Its science the most extensive of any. viz. Commodities, Trades, Provisions, Shipbuilding, Discipline, Winds, Tides,

Seas, Climates, Accounts, Thrift,
Seamanship, Navigation, Sea-Laws etc.
No one man qualified for all. Nor fit to be
trusted alone. Therefore the old
Constitution [i.e. the Navy Board]
provided for all and by a plurality
properly qualified.

Rawl A 170, f. 217

I find several contracts of theirs [i.e. the
Commonwealth] wherein it was expressly
covenanted for the Merchant to have his
money paid him at the Seal. What days
were those!

LBK, 524

If there be any English man of war in the
Bay of Cales or elsewhere, you may very
properly, as an English gentleman in your
travell, make your visites to them and their
ships; you will be sure to learn something
or other of them. And if you let them know
your relation to me, if they be old
commanders they will probably show you
respect, or greatly forget themselves. If
they be younkers, and so may not have
had to do with me, you will at least (as
before) have something or other new to
observe, and that's worth your visit, be it
good or bad.

PC, i.359

I have your letter of 12th instant, and could not have believed the method of my proceedings in the Navy could, after near twenty years observation, be so ill understood by any one man therein as it seems to have been done by you, when you would think any offer of money or any other argument can obtain anything from me that bare virtue cannot. But all the amends I shall take for the wrong you have done me in it is to let you remain under your mistake concerning, your very loving friend.

FC, 329

Sir W. Booth and Mr Sheres do agree with me that gentlemen ought to be brought into the Navy, as being men that are more sensible of honour than a man of meaner birth (though here may be room to examine whether as great actions in honour have not been done by plain seamen, and as mean by gentlemen as any others, and this is worthy enquiry) but then they ought to be brought up by times at sea … to everything. And then besides the good they would do for King and Navy, by their friends at Court they would themselves espouse the cause of the seamen and know what they deserve, and love them as part of himself ….

T, 122

The King's wages better than merchantmen's, and yet his service shunned by reason of bad pay [i.e. its arrears and irregularity].

NM, 24

The discipline among the French seamen and officers is extraordinary great compared with ours, which ought to be rectified by better payment and then stricter command.

NM, 38

Politics & Public Affairs

But Lord, the sorry talk and discourse
among the great courtiers round about him
[the King], without any reverence in the
world, but with so much disorder.

D. 26 October 1664

The King doth not concern himself to
relieve or justify anybody, but is wholly
negligent of everybody's concernment.

D. 9 December 1667

The House of Commons will never
ascertain their privileges nor be bound by
their orders; and yet expect the King
should.

NM, 3

No King ever did so unaccountable a thing
to oblige his people by, as to dissolve a
Commission of the Admiralty then in his
own hand, who best understands the
business of the sea of any prince the world
ever had, and things never better done,
and put it into hands which he knew were
wholly ignorant thereof, sporting himself
with their ignorance ...

NM, 71[*]

[*]On Charles II's dissolution in 1679 of the Admiralty
Commission he had appointed in 1673 see Richard Ollard,
Pepys (n.e. 1991), 292.

The Dominion of the Sea seems to have principally served for a ground for our princes to ask money upon, and for the people to reproach their princes with the decay of.

NM, 92

No larger provision is made for the representing the seamen in Parliament than was when all lay in the Cinque Ports, though both in war and peace the business and service of our Navy is become infinitely more than in those days.

NM, 136

The ale-conner an office more provided for in the law of England than a ship.

NM, 172

Our King's being a seaman has appeared rather to have rendered our navigation worse than better, by reason of our commanders and officers (especially gentlemen) finding so easy access and talk to him, and thereby insinuating things to and obtaining orders from him without being duly considered in their proper place, to the great contempt of his Officers of his Admiralty and Navy; especially where those of the Admiralty are so little knowing in the business of their office as they are now. Whereas where a king is wholly unskilful, he is the less apt to entertain motions upon that subject himself, but refers all to his proper ministers.

NM, 194

Though I had more reasons than most others, as having so many and great charges upon my hands without any written commission and acting under a Prince without any warrant than the word of his mouth, yet never did I, nor would be prevailed with to take out a pardon, though most of the greatest Ministers of State have and do, and particularly my Lord of Shaftesbury, and though I could have had it with as much ease and ask it upon better ground than any of them, considering the many points of consequence worthy collection and enumeration wherein I was concerned to do my office as Secretary of the Admiralty without any other justification than the King's verbal command. And yet in the greatest heat in Parliament, when my Lord Treasurer Danby, both the Secretaries of State, and other King's Ministers did all of them publicly in Parliament take to themselves the benefit of the King's name for their security in justifying their several managements, and thereby leaving upon the King (whether justly or unjustly I do not enquire) the answering whatever was thought amiss in the government, I did never, in the midst of all their persecutions and charges of mismanagement in the Navy, with their personal applications of the same to me under the envious name of Admiral, I say I did never once resort for my defence to the making use of the King's commands, but took upon myself at my own hazard the justifying every act that

had passed the Admiralty and Navy
through my hands from the true and
necessary reasons of it, and no other. And
this with such success as, when they found
themselves defeated of all just occasions of
censure upon me in my public capacity,
they were driven to serve themselves with
unjust ones in my private.

NM, 197-8

Marriage & Family Life

And thus till night, that our music came
and the office ready, and candles; and also
W. Batelier and his sister Susan came, and
also Will How and two gentlemen more,
strangers, which at my request yesterday
he did bring to dance, called Mr Ireton and
Mr Starkey; we fell to dancing and
continued, only with intermission for a
good supper, till 2 in the morning, the
music being Greeting and another most
excellent violin and theorbo, the best in
town; and so, with mighty mirth and
pleased with their dancing of jiggs
afterward, several of them, and among
others Betty Turner, who did mighty
prettily; and lastly, W. Batelier's blackmore
and blackmore-maid, and then to a
country-dance again; and so broke up with
extraordinary pleasure, as being one of the
days and nights of my life spent with the
greatest content, and that I can but hope to
repeat again a few times in my whole life.

D, 2 March 1669

I went by water home, where I was angry
with my wife for her things lying about,
and in my passion kicked the little fine
baskett which I bought her in Holland and
broke it, which troubled me after I had
done it.

D, 13 October 1660

At night to bed; and my wife and I did fall out about the dog's being put down in the sellar, which I have a mind to have done because of his fouling the house; and I would have my will. And so we went to bed and lay all night in a quarrell. This night I was troubled all night with a dream that my wife was dead, which made me that I slept ill all night.   D, 6 November 1660

My wife and I home and find all well. Only, myself somewhat vexed at my wife's neglect of her scarfe, waistcoat, and night-dressings in the coach today that brought us from Westminster, though I confess she did give them to me to look after – yet it was her fault not to see that I did take them out of the coach.

D, 6 January 1663

This day by the blessing of God, my wife and I have been married nine years – but my head being full of business, I did not think of it, to keep it in any extraordinary manner. But bless God for our long lives and loves and health together, which the same God long continue, I wish from my very heart.   D, 10 October 1664

To church in the morning, and there saw a wedding in the church, which I have not seen many a day, and the young people so merry one with another; and strange, to see what delight we married people have to see these poor fools decoyed into our condition, every man and wife gazing and smiling at them.   D, Christmas Day 1665

Therefore do not expect that any professions of frugality can be of satisfaction to me but what appears in an account. Not but that I could wish with all my heart that my brother's condition and yours would afford you a larger allowance. But where every farthing of what he and you spend is to be taken up upon credit as it is without any surety of prospect when you will be in a condition to repay it and yet (besides all this) a numerous stock of children to provide for you ought not to think any degree of sparing too much to be exercised ....

FL, 188

This satisfaction I have as to your owne particular that I have discharged my part of friendship and care towards you and your Family, as farr as I have been, or could ever hope to be able, were I to live 20 yeares longer in the Navy; and to such a Degree, as will with your good Conduct, enable you both to provide well for your family and at the same time doe your King and Country good Service. Wherein I pray God to bless you soe, as that you may neither by any neglect or miscarriage fayle in the latter, nor by any improvidence (which I must declare to you I am most doubtfull of and in paine for) live to lament your neglect of my repeted admonitions to you touching the latter.

FL, 205

Money

For my becoming your security in matter of mony is a thing I have never given way to, in behalfe of my owne Brother, and therefore must entreate your excuseing my not doing it in any other's case.

Rawl A 178, f. 106

But it is a strange thing to observe, and fit for me to remember, that I am at no time so unwilling to part with money, as when I am concerned in the getting of it most (as, I thank God, of late I have got more in this month, *viz.* near 250*L*) than ever I did in half a year before in my life, I think.

D, 21 September 1664

Among other things, my Lady [Lady Sandwich] did mightily urge me to lay out money upon my wife, which I perceived was a little more earnest than ordinary; and so I seemed to be pleased with it and do resolve to bestow a lace upon her.

D, 9 November 1660

So to the Wardrobe, where I find my Lady hath agreed upon a lace for my wife, of 6*L*., which I seemed much glad that it was no more, though in my mind I think it too much, and I pray God keep me so to order myself and my wife's expenses that no inconvenience in purse or honour follow this my prodigality.

D, 11 November 1660

All the afternoon to my accounts again;
and there find myself, to my great joy, a
great deal worth above 4000*L*, for which
the Lord be praised – and is principally
occasioned by my getting 500*L* of Cocke
for my profit in his bargain of prize goods,
and from Mr Gawden's making me a
present of 500*L* more when I paid him
8000*L* for Tanger.

D, 30 December 1665

Off to the Sun taverne with Sir W. Warren
and with him discoursed long and had
good advice and hints from him; and
among [other] things, he did give me a
pair of gloves for my wife, wrapped up in
paper; which I would not open, feeling it
hard, but did tell him my wife should
thank him, and so went on in discourse.
When I came home, Lord, in what pain I
was to get my wife out of the room
without bidding her go, that I might see
what these gloves were; and by and by, she
being gone, it proves a pair of white gloves
for her and 40 pieces in good gold; which
did so cheer my heart I could eat no
victuals almost for dinner for joy to think
how God doth bless us every day more
and more – and more yet I hope he will
upon the encrease of my duty and
endeavours.

D, 2 February 1664

This night I received by Will 105*L* – the first fruits of my endeavours in the late contract for victualling of Tanger – for which God be praised. For I can with a safe conscience say that I have therein saved the King 5000*L* per annum, and yet got myself a hope of 300*L* per annum without the least wrong to the King. So to supper and to bed.

D, 10 September 1664

Writing Letters

My late silence has been the muchness of my other business and the little I have had to say to you.

Rawl. A 193, f. 208

Pray therefore let us have no more of this sort of correspondence between us, for as I am one too stubborn ever knowingly to endure being imposed upon, so shall I with much less willingness be ever provoked to violate the known simplicity of my dealings, especially with one from whom I shall always own my having received such civilities as may challenge and shall meet with all expression of gratitude on this side admitting of a manifest wrong.

Rawl. A 172, f. 107

Length is no commendation to a letter from him that has nothing to doe to you that have a great deal.

PC, i.109

That which I labour most to merit by – I mean the easiness, civility and dispatch which I pretend to give … to all that have occasion of applications to my office.

FC, 290

It is at the importunity of a very good
friend of mine and one known to yourself,
Mr Cooling, that I give you this trouble, in
a matter wherein I wish myself as well able
to judge what to ask, as I should be ready
to ask anything wherein I might express
my respect to him. But to tell you the truth,
I am wholly at a loss in the matter wherein
he calls for my present help, which is the
moving you in what I presume he will be
more particular in to you by a letter from
himself, to permit the bearer, a son of his,
to pass his time on board you this voyage;
one on whom he has bestowed a very
liberal and generous education, but with
so much liberty allowed or taken by him,
that I find him got beyond the power of his
father to confine him to any of those
employments on shore for which he has
qualified him; his addiction seeming to be
immoveably bent to the sea, though
without any better inducement (I fear) to it
than the expectation of his being thereby
further removed from restraint and
business, insomuch that I have with the
freedom of a friend given it his father as
my opinion that the sending him to sea
must in all likelihood prove the delivering
him up to a stronger habit of liberty and
idleness, without the least hopes within
my view of his being in any respect
rendered better by it. However, my friend
his father, not so much from his being of
any better belief, but his want of knowing
how to divert his son from this fancy of his
to the sea, is pleased to insist upon my

letter to you so far only as may signify my
concurrence with his desire to you of
giving him (as I have said) his bare
passage with you, telling me that he will
be answerable to your full satisfaction for
whatever trouble or charge shall arise to
you from it.

FC, 322-3

Descriptive Reporting

I went up to the Lobby, where I saw the
Speaker reading of a letter [from General
Monck, demanding the re-admission of the
Secluded Members, which would make the
Restoration of the Monarchy a certainty] …
and after it was read, Sir A. Haslerig came
out very angry. Hence I went alone to
Guildhall to see whether Monck was come
yet or no, and met him coming out of the
chamber where he had been with the
Mayor and Aldermen; but such a shout I
have never heard in all my life, crying out
'God bless your Excellence!' And endeed I
saw many people give the soldiers drink
and money, and all along in the streets
cried, 'God bless them!' and extraordinary
good words. In Cheapside there were a
great many bonefires, and Bow bells and
all the bells in all the churches as we went
home were aringing. Hence we went
homewards, it being about 10 a-clock. But
the common joy that was everywhere to be
seen! The number of bonefires – there
being fourteen between St Dunstan's and
Temple Bar. And at Strand Bridge I could
at one view tell 31 fires. In King Streete,
seven or eight; and all along burning and
roasting and drinking for rumps – there
being rumps tied upon sticks and carried
up and down. The butchers at the Maypole
in the Strand rang a peal with their knives

when they were going to sacrifice their
rump. On Ludgate Hill there was one
turning of the spit, that had a rump tied
upon it, and another basting of it. Indeed it
was past imagination, both the greatness
and the suddenness if it. At one end of the
street, you would think there was a whole
lane of fire, and so hot that we were fain to
keep still on the further side merely for
heat.   D, 11 February 1660

The absence of the Court and emptiness of
the city takes away all occasion of news,
save only such melancholy stories as
would rather sadden than find your
Ladyship any divertisement in the hearing;
I having stayed in the city till above 7400
died in one week, and of them above 6000
of the plague, and little noise heard day or
night but tolling of bells; till I could walk
Lumber street* and not meet twenty
persons from one end to the other, and not
fifty upon the Exchange; till whole families
(ten and twelve together) have been swept
away; till my very physician, Dr Burnet,
who undertook to secure me against any
infection (having survived the month of
his own being shut up) died himself of the
plague; till the nights (though much
lengthened) are grown too short to conceal
the burials of those that died the day
before, people being thereby constrained
to borrow daylight for that service; lastly,
till I could find neither meat nor drink safe,
the butcheries being everywhere visited,

* Lombard Street.

my brewer's house shut up, and my baker with his whole family dead of the plague.

Howarth, 24-5

So down, with my heart full of trouble, to the Lieutenant of the Tower, who tells me that it begun this morning in the King's bakers house in Pudding Lane, and that it hath burned down St Magnes Church and most part of Fish Streete already. So I down to the waterside and there got a boat and through the bridge, and there saw a lamentable fire. Poor Michells house, as far as the Old Swan, already burned that way and the fire running further, that in a very little time it got as far as the Stillyard while I was there. Everybody endeavouring to remove their goods, and flinging into the river or bringing them into lighters that lay off. Poor people staying in their houses as long as till the very fire touched them, and then running into boats or clambering from one pair of stair by the waterside to another. And among other things, the poor pigeons I perceive were loath to leave their houses, but hovered about the windows and balconies till they were some of them burned, their wings, and fell down.

Having stayed, and in an hour's time seen the fire rage every way, and nobody to my sight endeavouring to quench it, but to remove their goods and leave all to the fire; and having seen it get as far as the Steeleyard, and the wind mighty high and driving it into the City, and everything, after so long a drought, proving

combustible, even the very stones of
churches ... I go to Whitehall ... and word
was carried in to the King, so I was called
for and did tell the King and Duke of York
what I saw, and that unless his Majesty did
command houses to be pulled down,
nothing could stop the fire.

D, 2 September 1666

History

Memoirs are true and useful stars, whilst studied histories are those stars joined in constellations, according to the fancy of the poet.

NM, 69

There seems to have been a spirit extraordinary stirring among our nobility and gentry in Queen Elizabeth's time towards the sea, beyond what appears to have been ever before or since; imputable, I think, to their then fervour for religion and against Spain, joined with the general better morals of that age than usual.

NM, 215

Walked with Mr Coventry to St James's. After dinner, we did talk of a History of the Navy of England, how fit it were to be writ; and he did say that it hath been in his mind to propose to me the writing of the history of the late Dutch warr [of 1652-4] – which I am glad to hear, it being a thing I much desire and sorts mightily with my genius – and if done well, may recommend me much. So he says he will get me an order for making of searches to all records &c. in order thereto, and I shall take great delight in doing of it.

D, 13 June 1664

To the second Earl of Clarendon. 4 August 1702

My Lord, I am but this morning come from the 3rd reading of your noble Father my Lord Chancellor Clarendon's History with the same appetite (I assure you) to a 4th that ever I had to the first; it being plain that that great story neither had nor could ever have been told as it ought to bee but by that hand and spirit that has now done it, or (I hope) soon will, and that your Lordship therefore, and my honoured Lord your Brother [Laurence Hyde, Earl of Rochester], won't suffer the press to slacken in the dispatch of the remainder, and therewith in the eternizing the honour of your name and family, the delivering your country from the otherwise endless consequences of that its depraved loyalty which nothing but this can cure, and your putting together such a Lecture of Government for an English Prince as I won't distrust but you may yet live to bee thankt and to thank God for.

PC, ii.266

It seems a little hard that never any admiral nor Secretary of the Admiralty nor sea commander should ever write a history of our Navy matters, but that we must owe all we have to a poor private minister Hakluyt.

T, 148

Patriotism & National Character

The nature of the English is generally to be self-lovers, and thinking everything of their own the best, viz. our beef, beer, women, horses, religion, laws, etc., and from the same principles are over-valuers of our ships.

NM, 2

What a wonder we made of Sir Francis Drake's vessel, when the same voyage had been gone twice before by others!

NM, 85

My sister St Michel living long in Holland and at Deal, has observed to me that the Dutch seamen are ever better clad than ours, and either are soberer or can bear drink better. And it is notorious how much neater they generally live on shipboard than we.

NM, 86

Was there not ignorance more than knowledge, courage or force in our first assuming to ourselves the Dominion of the sea?

NM, 226

Is there any country in the World where the usage to persons and goods shipwrecked is more or less cruel than in England?

T, 166

Illness & Old Age

I remember not my life without the pain of the stone in the kidneys (even to the making of bloody water upon any extraordinary motion) till I was about 20 years of age, when upon drinking an extraordinary quantity of conduit-water out of Aristotle's well near Cambridge (where some scholars of us were for refreshment in a hot summer's day walked), the weight of the said water carried after some day's pain the stone out of the kidneys more sensibly through the ureter into the bladder, from which moment I lived under a constant succession of fits of stone in the bladder till I was about 26 years of age when the pain growing insupportable I was delivered both of it and the stone by cutting and continued free from both (by God's blessing) to this day, more than what may be imputed to it of the aptness which I still retain to cold and wind and the pain attending the same in those parts.

Rawl A 185, f. 210

To acquaint you that it has been my calamity for much the greatest part of this time [four weeks] to have been kept bed-rid under an evil so rarely known as to have had it made a matter of universal surprise, and with little less general

opinion of its dangerousness: namely, that
the cicatrice of a wound occasioned upon
my cutting for the stone, without hearing
any thing of it in all this time, should after
more than fourty-year-perfect cure, all on a
sudden, without any known occasion
given for it, break-out againe, so as to
make another issue for my urine to sally at,
besides that of its natural channel. A thing
(as I have sayd before) never till now
heard-of, and calling for an operation for
its cure every whit as extraordinary, by
requiring the wound that has been so long
asleep to be a-new layd open again and
re-healed, which it has been, and after that
a second time; but both unsuccessfully. But
I have great hopes given mee that what has
been since done upon the third breach will
prove thoroughly effectual; I being (I thank
God) once more upon my legs, and though
my long lying in bed will cost me possibly
some time for the removal of my
weakness, yet I am in no doubt of
recovering my first state very soon ....

PC, i.316-17

It was not without very much ground that
in one of my late letters of generall advice
to you, I cautioned you against depending
upon any support much longer from mee,
I then feeling what I cannot hide, I mean,
that paine which I at this day labour under
(night and day) from a new Stone lodged
in my kidneys and an ulcer attending it,
with a generall decay of my Stomack and

Strength, that cannot be playd with long,
nor am I solicitous that it should.

FL, 205

All which trouble, past and to com, pray,
gentlemen, lett your Father (to whome my
many servisses) bare the blame of, for not
keeping his word in makeing this toure
long agoe with me himselfe; till now that
another tour atends us boath that will call
for a much greater preparation (god help
us in it) than we could ever have needed
for a tripp to Rome.

PC, i.247

I am sated with the world, and am within
little of being praevayled with by my
physician and friends (my nearest
councellers for my health) to bid so farr an
adieu to't as to sett up the short remainder
of my rest here where I now am, without
troubling the towne or my selfe with it
more.

PC, i.356

Dearest Sir – *Dover Streete* at the topp and *J.
Evelyn* at the bottom had alone been a sight
equal in the pleasure of it to all I have had
before me in my 2 or 3 months by-work. ...
   What then should I have to say to the
whole of that glorious matter that was so
enclosed in your last? Why truly, neither
more nor lesse than it looks to me like a
seraphick *How d'ye* from one already
entred into the regions you talk of in it,
and who has sent me this for a *Viaticum*
toward my speeding thither after him.

PC, ii.241